cutting board

potato peeler

hand mixer

mason jar

D0573034

whisk

Measurement Guide

tsp.	teaspoon
tbsp.	tablespoon
c.	cup
oz.	ounce
lb.	pound

COOL KIDS COOK

"Kid Chef Eliana is a very gifted young chef. I love how she expresses her love for food and cooking, which reveals her heritage, passion, and her creativity. She is an inspiration for all, with each dish showing us that dreams can really become a reality when you put your heart into something you love."
—José Andrés, chef, author, and restaurateur

Kid Chef Eliana grew up in a family of cooks. With grandparents from Cajun Louisiana, the Philippines, Cuba, and Honduras, Eliana's recipes have international flair and feature fresh, local produce and ingredients.

As a young child, Kid Chef Eliana was chosen as one of thirteen Latinos profiled in a museum exhibit at the Southern Food and Beverage Museum in New Orleans. Featured in the "Top 10 Most Famous Kid Critics and Cooks" in the world by *The Daily Meal,* Kid Chef Eliana is also the youngest person ever named a 40 Under 40 mover and shaker by *Gambit.* She has met, interviewed, and cooked with celebrity chefs across the country. Her mission is to educate kids and inspire them to become culinary explorers. Her motto is "Cool kids cook and get creative in the kitchen!"

In praise of **Cool Kids Cook: Louisiana:**

"Kid Chef Eliana is an inspiration to kid and adult chefs alike and in **Cool Kids Cook,** her passion shines through."
—Chef John Besh, author of *My New Orleans* and *My Family Table*

"Eliana is a very talented young girl. She represents the new generation of chefs—who's passionate about where she's from and where she's going."
—Chef Aarón Sanchez, author and co-star of Food Network's *Heat Seekers* and *Chopped*

"This Cool Cookbook is for anyone who loves the flavors and aromas of down-home Louisiana cooking."
—Chef LaLa, chef, nutritionist, and author of *Yummy for Your Tummy*

COOL KIDS COOK

Fresh & Fit

By Kid Chef Eliana

with Dianne de Las Casas

Illustrated by Soleil Lisette

PELICAN PUBLISHING COMPANY

GRETNA 2014

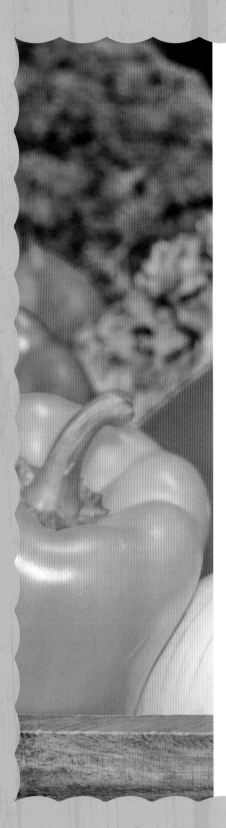

Introduction

Hey, Young Chefs!

I'm excited to bring you this cookbook full of healthy recipes inspired by global cuisine. I love trying new foods, especially ones that are fresh and seasonal. These dishes are delicious and fun, too.

Miso Chicken Lettuce Wraps combine my love of Japanese and Vietnamese foods. Pesto is a summer favorite in my family, and we grow our own basil. The roasted flavor of the Brussels Sprout Salad makes the veggies so yummy. If you love potato chips, you will be amazed by how crunchy and delicious my Vinegar and Sea Salt Kale Chips are! For those of you with a sweet tooth, try the Fresh Fruit Tart or the Inside-Out Peach Crumble. Mmm!

The cookbook begins with basics that are the foundation for many of the recipes in this book. The cooking utensils you will need as well as an abbreviation guide for measurements are included in the front and back endpapers. Definitions for unfamiliar cooking terms are located in the glossary at the end of the book.

Balance your meals with lean proteins, vegetables, fruit, whole grains, and dairy. If you need some guidance, look for organizations that give recommendations and tips for creating healthy meals. Staying fit also means getting exercise and staying active. I have included "Fit Tips" with each recipe to help you get started. See how you can make a difference in your family's life! Cool kids cook and get fresh and fit!

Bon Appétit!

Kid Chef Eliana

Italian Soffritto (soh-FREE-toe)
Makes about 2 cups

Ingredients

2 large cloves garlic
1 large onion
2 medium stalks celery

Directions

1. Dice all ingredients.
2. Place in a medium bowl and mix well.
3. Store in an airtight container in the refrigerator for up to three days.

Seasoning Salt
Makes 1½ cups

Ingredients

2 tbsp. salt
2 tbsp. onion powder
2 tbsp. garlic powder
2 tbsp. dried oregano
2 tbsp. dried sweet basil
2 tbsp. dried marjarom

1 tbsp. dried thyme
½ tbsp. black pepper
½ tbsp. white pepper
1 tbsp. celery seed
1 tbsp. ground cumin
5 tbsp. sweet paprika

Directions

1. Mix all ingredients thoroughly in a large bowl.
2. Store in spice bottle or jar.

Twenty-Minute Tomato Sauce
Makes about 2 cups

Ingredients

½ c. soffritto (see Basics)
1 tbsp. olive oil
2 large whole tomatoes, diced
2 tbsp. tomato paste
1 tbsp. Italian seasoning

1 tsp. fresh parsley, chopped
1 tsp. salt
¼ tsp. black pepper
½ c. water
1 tbsp. honey

Directions

1. In a medium saucepan over medium heat, sauté soffritto in olive oil until translucent.
2. Add remaining ingredients. Mix well and simmer for 10 minutes.
3. Using an immersion blender or food processor, blend the sauce until smooth and thick.

Vinaigrette (vin-uh-GRET)
Makes 1 cup

Chef's Note

I love this quick and easy tomato sauce. It's very versatile! My dad and I use it on homemade pizzas. My mom and I use it with pastas. We always have some stashed in the freezer.

Ingredients

¼ c. balsamic vinegar
¾ c. olive oil
2 tsp. honey

1 tsp. garlic, minced
½ tsp. salt
½ tsp. black pepper

Directions

1. Place all ingredients in a glass or Mason jar, and secure the lid.
2. Shake, shake, shake!
3. Use immediately or store in the refrigerator.

TOMATOES

BASIL

ROMAINE

BEETS

Main Dishes

Beef and Broccoli Stir-fry	10
Blackened Chicken Tacos	13
Coconut Shrimp	14
Creole Pasta Primavera	17
Curry Fish Taco Salad	18
Eggplant Lasagna	21
Greektalian Chicken Kebabs	22
Grilled Chicken Satay	25
Miso Chicken Lettuce Wraps	26
Pasta Bolognese	29
Pesto Chicken Sandwich	30
Super-Moist Turkey Burger	33

CELERY

Beef and Broccoli Stir-fry
Serves 4

Ingredients

4 tbsp. soy sauce
1/2 tsp. sesame oil
2 tbsp. orange marmalade
1 tsp. honey
2/3 c. water
1 tsp. ginger, grated

8 oz. flank steak, cut into strips
3 c. broccoli florets, blanched
   and shocked
2 tsp. cornstarch

Directions

1. In a medium bowl, mix soy sauce, sesame oil, marmalade, honey, water, and ginger. Set aside half the marinade.
2. Using half the marinade, marinate flank steak for 15 minutes.
3. Remove steak from marinade and cook in a wok over medium-high heat until steak is no longer pink.
4. Add broccoli. Stir-fry for 5 minutes.
5. Mix cornstarch into the reserved marinade. Pour sauce into wok and stir until sauce is thickened.

Chef's Note

I love Chinese take-out. This dish is much healthier and cooks up quickly!

fit Tip

Ride a bike!

Beef and Broccoli Stir-Fry

Blackened Chicken Tacos

Blackened Chicken Tacos
Serves 4

Ingredients

1 lb. chicken breast
2 tbsp. Creole seasoning
  Olive oil spray
8 8" whole wheat tortillas,
  warmed

1 head lettuce, chopped
2 c. salsa
½ c. cheddar cheese, grated

Directions

1. Coat chicken with Creole seasoning.
2. Coat chicken breast with olive oil spray on all sides.
3. Spray a medium-sized cast-iron skillet with olive oil spray. Heat on high until skillet is very hot.
4. Using tongs, place chicken in the hot pan. Cook until dark brown on both sides, about 4-5 minutes per side.
5. Let rest for 5 minutes and cut into ½"-thick strips.
6. Place strips inside warm tortilla shells and layer with lettuce, salsa, and cheese.

Chef's Note

Traditional blackening is done with butter. This technique is lighter and healthier but still full of flavor.

Coconut Shrimp
Serves 4-6

Ingredients

Non-stick cooking spray
½ c. dry, shredded coconut
2 c. panko bread crumbs
½ tsp. ground ginger
½ tsp. salt
½ tsp. white pepper

2 egg whites, beaten
18-24 large tail-on shrimp, cleaned and butterflied

Directions

1. Preheat oven to 425 degrees. Grease a cookie sheet with non-stick cooking spray.
2. In a large bowl, mix coconut, bread crumbs, ginger, salt, and pepper.
3. Place egg whites in a separate bowl. Dip shrimp in egg whites, followed by coconut mixture.
4. Place shrimp on a greased cookie sheet and lightly spray shrimp with cooking spray.
5. Bake shrimp for 7½ minutes per side for a total baking time of 15 minutes.

Chef's Note

This Coconut Shrimp is so flavorful. If you want a quick dipping sauce, mix 2 tbsp. plum jam with 2 tbsp. rice vinegar and a pinch of dried chili flakes. Yum!

Coconut Shrimp

Creole Pasta Primavera

Creole Pasta Primavera (PREE-mah-VEH-rah)
Serves 8-10

Ingredients

1 c. soffritto (see Basics)	1 c. shiitake mushrooms, chopped
½ bell pepper, chopped	1 tbsp. Creole seasoning
2 tbsp. olive oil	Salt to taste
1½ c. baby yellow squash, thinly sliced	1 lb. whole wheat rotini, cooked according to package directions
1½ c. baby zucchini, thinly sliced	¼ c. Asiago cheese, grated
2 tomatoes, diced	

Directions

1. In a large pot over medium-high heat, sauté soffritto and bell pepper in olive oil for 5 minutes.
2. Add squash, zucchini, tomatoes, mushrooms, Creole seasoning, and salt.
3. Cook for 7 minutes or until tender.
4. Stir in rotini and Asiago.

Chef's Note

Primavera means "spring" in Spanish and Italian. This dish celebrates spring veggies. I invented it at a cooking demo for the Crescent City Farmers Market in New Orleans using farm-fresh produce and cheese.

Curry Fish Taco Salad
Serves 4

Ingredients

1 tbsp. curry powder
1 c. Greek yogurt
1 tsp. salt
½ tsp. pepper
4 4-oz. mild white fish
   fillets

Lettuce, for serving
Tomatoes, for serving
4 tortilla bowls

Directions

1. Preheat oven to 350 degrees.
2. In a medium bowl, mix curry powder, yogurt, salt, and pepper. Add fish fillets to bowl and stir to coat.
3. Make a packet out of aluminum foil and seal fish inside. Bake for 15 minutes or until fish is cooked through.
4. Place lettuce and tomatoes in each tortilla bowl. Place fish on top and serve.

Chef's Note

This is a "wet" curry because yogurt is added to the curry powder. Curry powder is actually a combination of many spices, including paprika, turmeric, cumin, ginger, coriander, cardamom, and pepper.

Curry Fish Taco Salad

Eggplant Lasagna

Eggplant Lasagna (luh-ZAHN-yuh)

Serves 6-8

Ingredients

Salt to taste
2 large eggplants, sliced ¼" thick
1 c. soffritto (see Basics)
1 tbsp. olive oil
1 lb. ground turkey
1 tbsp. seasoning salt (see Basics)
2 c. twenty-minute tomato
    sauce (see Basics)

3 c. fresh baby spinach
2 c. fat-free ricotta cheese
5 c. low-fat mozzarella cheese, grated
1½ c. Parmesan cheese, grated, divided
4 egg whites

Directions

1. Preheat oven to 375 degrees.
2. Lightly salt eggplant slices on both sides and let sit 15 minutes. Rinse and pat dry. Set aside.
3. In a large skillet over medium-high heat, sauté soffritto in olive oil until onions are translucent.
4. Add ground turkey; brown the meat. Add seasoning salt and mix thoroughly.
5. Add tomato sauce and reduce heat to medium-low. Simmer for 10 minutes.
6. Add spinach and cook until completely wilted.
7. In a large bowl, combine ricotta cheese, mozzarella cheese, 1 cup Parmesan cheese, and egg whites.
8. In a 9" x 12" greased casserole dish, spread a layer of sauce over the bottom of the pan. Layer eggplant over sauce. Spread some of the cheese mixture on top of eggplant. Spread a layer of sauce over cheese. Continue layering eggplant, cheese, and sauce until dish is full.
9. Sprinkle remaining ½ cup Parmesan cheese on top, cover with foil, and bake for 45 minutes. Let rest 15 minutes before serving.

Chef's Note

This is a fantastic family meal that is healthy and tasty. It's just like regular lasagna, except it's better for you!

Greektalian Chicken Kebabs

Serves 6-8

Ingredients

2 lbs. chicken breast, cut into 1"-thick strips
¼ c. olive oil
¼ c. white wine vinegar
1 tbsp. Greek seasoning
1 tbsp. Italian seasoning

Directions

1. Place chicken in a large re-sealable plastic bag. Add remaining ingredients and seal the bag.
2. Shake bag to coat chicken thoroughly, and marinate for 30 minutes.
3. Skewer chicken onto kebab sticks and grill both sides until chicken is cooked, about 15 minutes.

Chef's Note

These kebabs are fabulous for a party. I make these kebabs for family gatherings, and everyone loves them. They go really well with the Chèvre Pear Salad, too. Mmm!

Greektalian Chicken Kebabs

Grilled Chicken Satay

Grilled Chicken Satay (sah-TAY)

Serves 4-6

Ingredients

4 tbsp. peanut butter
4 tbsp. sesame oil
4 tsp. soy sauce
    Juice of 1 lime
1 c. orange juice

2 tsp. rice vinegar
1 lb. chicken breast,
    cut into 1"-thick strips

Directions

1. Mix peanut butter, sesame oil, soy sauce, lime juice, orange juice, and rice vinegar in a food processor until well combined. Reserve half the sauce.
2. With the remaining sauce, coat chicken and marinate for 30 minutes.
3. Place chicken on soaked skewers and grill both sides until chicken is cooked through, about 15 minutes.
4. Serve with reserved peanut sauce.

Chef's Note

Satay originated in Indonesia. It is a national dish that also has become popular in other Asian countries, including Singapore, Malaysia, Thailand, and the Philippines.

Miso Chicken Lettuce Wraps (ME-so)

Serves 4-6

Ingredients

4 tbsp. miso paste
2 tbsp. freshly grated ginger
1 tbsp. lemongrass paste
1 c. rice vinegar
½ c. sesame oil
2 cloves garlic, minced
3 extra-large boneless, skinless chicken breasts

1 bunch butter or romaine lettuce
1 carrot, julienned
1 daikon radish, julienned
Fresh mint, basil, and/or cilantro, for serving

Directions

1. In a medium bowl, mix together miso paste, ginger, lemongrass paste, rice vinegar, sesame oil, and garlic. Pour into a re-sealable plastic bag.
2. Add the chicken to the bag and seal well. Marinate chicken overnight in the fridge.
3. Before cooking, allow chicken to come to room temperature.
4. Grill on both sides over medium-high heat, about 15 minutes.
5. Allow chicken to rest for 5 minutes, then cut into 1"-thick strips.
6. Break off whole leaves of lettuce and arrange so that the leaves form cups. To serve, place chicken, carrot, radish, and herbs into lettuce cups.

Chef's Note

Miso is a Japanese seasoning paste traditionally made from soybeans. Its saltiness adds tremendous flavor. For a delicious dipping sauce for the wraps, mix equal parts mango jam and rice vinegar.

Miso Chicken Lettuce Wraps

Pasta Bolognese

Pasta Bolognese (bowl-oh-NYEH-zeh)

Serves 6-8

Ingredients

1 tbsp. olive oil
1 c. soffritto (see Basics)
1 lb. lean ground beef
1 tbsp. seasoning salt
  (see Basics)
½ tsp. salt

2 c. twenty-minute tomato sauce
  (see Basics)
½ tsp. red pepper flakes
½ c. Parmesan cheese, grated
1 lb. whole wheat linguine, cooked
  according to package directions

Directions

1. In a large sauté pan, heat olive oil over medium heat. Add soffritto and sauté until translucent.
2. Add ground meat and brown, breaking apart meat until there are no large clumps. Add seasoning salt and salt, and mix well.
3. Add tomato sauce, red pepper flakes, and Parmesan cheese. Mix well.
4. Reduce heat to medium-low and cook for another 15 minutes, stirring occasionally.
5. Serve over linguine.

Chef's Note

Pasta Bolognese is a meat-based sauce that comes from Bologna, Italy. If you like spaghetti with meat sauce, then you will definitely like this.

Pesto Chicken Sandwich

Serves 4

Ingredients

3 c. fresh basil
$\frac{1}{3}$ c. Parmesan cheese, grated
$\frac{1}{4}$ cup fat-free, low-sodium chicken stock
2 tbsp. pine nuts
1 tbsp. extra virgin olive oil
$\frac{1}{2}$ tsp. salt

$\frac{1}{4}$ tsp. white pepper
1 garlic clove, minced
2 large chicken breasts, filleted
8 slices whole wheat bread
4 leaves lettuce
1 large tomato, sliced

Directions

1. Combine basil, Parmesan, chicken stock, pine nuts, olive oil, salt, pepper, and garlic in a food processor and blend until smooth.
2. Coat chicken breasts with half of the pesto and grill on both sides until cooked in the center.
3. Spread remaining pesto on 4 slices of bread and assemble sandwich with chicken, lettuce, and tomato slices.

Chef's Note

I love traditional pesto, but it has a lot of olive oil. This version lightens up a standard recipe by substituting tasty chicken stock.

Pesto Chicken Sandwich

Super-Moist Turkey Burger

Super-Moist Turkey Burger

Makes 4 burgers

Ingredients

1 c. soffritto (see Basics)
2 c. mushrooms
2 tbsp. olive oil
2 tbsp. seasoning salt
1 lb. ground turkey

4 hamburger buns
Lettuce, for serving
Tomatoes, for serving
Favorite condiments,
for serving

Directions

1. In a medium sauté pan, sauté soffritto and mushrooms in olive oil for 5 minutes.
2. Blend soffritto, mushrooms, and seasoning salt in a food processor until it becomes a paste.
3. In a large bowl, mix mushroom paste with ground turkey.
4. Form mixture into 4 patties and grill until cooked through.
5. Place one patty on each bun and top with lettuce, tomatoes, and your favorite condiments.

Chef's Note

This is a healthy burger that tastes good. The mushrooms keep the burgers moist and help them stay together.

Side Dishes

Baked Sweet Potato with Cinnamon Cream	36
Brussels Sprout Salad	39
Chèvre Pear Salad	40
Crab-Stuffed Tomatoes	43
Quinoa-Stuffed Peppers	44
Roasted Beets with Minted Yogurt	47
Vinegar and Sea Salt Kale Chips	48

Baked Sweet Potato with Cinnamon Cream

Serves 4

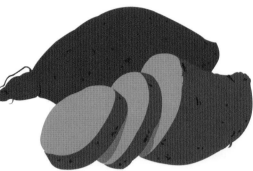

Ingredients

  4 small sweet potatoes
$1\frac{1}{2}$ c. fat-free vanilla yogurt
  2 tbsp. honey
  1 tsp. cinnamon

Directions

1. Preheat oven to 350 degrees.
2. Wrap each sweet potato in aluminum foil and bake for 1 hour and 15 minutes, or until soft.
3. While sweet potatoes are baking, mix yogurt, honey, and cinnamon in a large bowl.
4. When sweet potatoes are cooked, cut a slit down the middle and spoon cream inside.

Chef's Note

Cinnamon-honey butter is awesome on baked sweet potatoes. This uses the same concept but is healthier.

fit Tip

Sweep and mop!

Baked Sweet Potato with Cinnamon Cream

Brussels Sprout Salad

Brussels Sprout Salad

Serves 6-8

Ingredients

4 c. Brussels sprouts, sliced
1/8 c. olive oil
1/2 tsp. salt
1/2 tsp. black pepper
1/2 c. walnuts, chopped
1/2 c. strawberries, quartered

1/4 c. low-fat feta cheese, crumbled
Vinaigrette to taste (see Basics)
1 tsp. lemon zest

Directions

1. Preheat oven to 400 degrees. Line and grease a baking sheet
2. In a large bowl, toss Brussels sprouts in olive oil, salt, and pepper.
3. Place Brussels sprouts on prepared baking sheet and roast for 20 minutes.
4. In a large bowl, mix the roasted Brussels sprouts and remaining ingredients.

Chef's Note

Brussels sprouts grow on a stalk. They are high in Vitamin c and iron. They are delicious and this recipe has tons of flavor. For even more flavor, add 2 tbsp. honey and 1 tsp. lemon juice to 1/4 c. basic vinaigrette.

Chèvre Pear Salad (SHEV-rih)
Serves 4

Ingredients

3 c. mixed spring greens
2 Asian pears, diced
4 tbsp. chèvre, crumbled
4 tbsp. vinaigrette (see Basics)
1 tbsp. fig preserves
   Chopped walnuts, for serving

Directions

1. In a small bowl, toss together the greens, pears, and chèvre.
2. In another small bowl, whisk together the vinaigrette and fig preserves.
3. Drizzle the vinaigrette mixture over the salad. Sprinkle with walnuts.

Chef's Note

Chèvre, a creamy goat's cheese, is one of my favorite cheeses. If you don't like walnuts, use pine nuts or pecans instead.

fit Tip

Play at a playground!

Chèvre Pear Salad

Crab-Stuffed Tomatoes

Crab-Stuffed Tomatoes

Serves 6-8

Ingredients

1 8-oz. pkg. fat-free cream cheese, softened
1/4 c. fat-free mayonnaise
3 tbsp. milk
1 tsp. seasoning salt (see Basics)
1 tbsp. fresh parsley, chopped, plus additional for garnish

1/2 tsp. salt
12 oz. shredded, cooked crab
4 large tomatoes, hollowed out

Directions

1. In a bowl, combine cream cheese, mayonnaise, milk, seasoning salt, parsley, and salt.
2. Gently fold in crab.
3. Stuff crab mixture into tomatoes.
4. Garnish with fresh parsley.

Chef's Note

This is a cold dish that is great during the summer. It is perfect for picnics and outdoor parties—just be sure to keep the stuffed tomatoes on ice.

Quinoa-Stuffed Peppers (keen-WAH)
Serves 4

Ingredients

4 large bell peppers according

½ c. soffritto (see Basics)
1 tbsp. olive oil
2 tbsp. seasoning salt
½ c. pine nuts

2 c. quinoa, cooked to package directions
½ c. Asiago cheese, grated, divided

Directions

1. Preheat oven to 350 degrees.
2. Cut off the tops of the bell peppers and remove the ribs.
3. In a medium sauté pan, sauté soffritto in olive oil until tender.
4. In a large bowl, combine soffritto with seasoning salt, pine nuts, quinoa, and ¼ cup Asiago cheese.
5. Scoop mixture evenly into bell peppers and top with remaining ¼ cup Asiago.
6. Place bell peppers in a small casserole dish and bake for 30 minutes.

Chef's Note

Quinoa is a gluten-free whole grain with plenty of protein. This is a vegetarian dish that everyone in the family will love. It has no meat, but it is still filling!

Fit Tip

Play tug-of-war!

Quinoa-Stuffed Peppers

Roasted Beets with Minted Yogurt

Roasted Beets with Minted Yogurt

Serves 6

Ingredients

For the Beets:
- 3 large beets, stems removed
- 1 tbsp. olive oil
- 1 tsp. salt
- ¼ tsp. white pepper

For the Yogurt:
- ½ c. Greek yogurt
- 1 tbsp. chopped mint
- 1 tbsp. honey
- ½ tsp. salt
- ½ tsp. white pepper

Directions

For the Beets:
1. Preheat oven to 400 degrees.
2. Place beets in a small casserole dish. Drizzle with olive oil and season with salt and pepper.
3. Bake for 1 hour, or until tender. Allow to cool
4. Peel skin with a vegetable peeler and cut into even slices.
5. Serve with Minted Yogurt.

For the Yogurt:
1. Thoroughly mix all ingredients in a small bowl.

Chef's Note

I love roasted beets. They are one of my favorite vegetables! You might want to wear gloves when peeling them, because their reddish-purple juices stain hands and clothes.

Vinegar and Sea Salt Kale Chips

Serves 4

Ingredients

½ c. olive oil
½ c. distilled white vinegar
1 tsp. fine sea salt
1 bunch kale

Directions

1. Preheat oven to 375 degrees.
2. In a large bowl, combine olive oil, vinegar, and sea salt.
3. Add kale and massage oil into the leaves.
4. Place on a lined baking sheet, making sure that the kale leaves do not touch each other. Bake for 7 to 10 minutes. Do not let the kale leaves brown, or they will be bitter. Kale should be crunchy.

Chef's Note

It's hard to believe that a green, leafy vegetable can taste as delicious as potato chips, but it's true! Try these crunchy chips for yourself.

Vinegar and Sea Salt Kale Chips

Desserts

Berrylicious Parfait	52
Fresh Fruit Tart	55
Fruit Salsa with Cinnamon Chips	56
Inside-Out Peach Crumble	59
Watermelon and Pineapple Pops	60

Berrylicious Parfait (par-FAY)
Serves 2

Ingredients

3 tbsp. honey, divided
2 c. Greek yogurt
½ c. blueberries
½ c. strawberries, quartered
½ c. raspberries
Fresh mint, for serving

Directions

1. Mix 1 tbsp. honey with Greek yogurt.
2. In a separate bowl, mix remaining 2 tbsp. honey with berries.
3. To serve, alternate layers of yogurt and berry mix in a parfait glass.
4. Garnish with a sprig of fresh mint.

Chef's Note

This makes such an easy and delicious dessert. It's also very pretty, making it perfect for company. This parfait is perfect for breakfast and an after-school snack too!

Berrylicious Parfait

Fresh Fruit Tart

fresh fruit Tart
Serves 8

Ingredients

1 8-oz. package fat-free
  cream cheese, softened
2 tbsp. honey
8 pre-made mini pie crusts
3 strawberries, sliced

1 kiwi, peeled and sliced
$\frac{1}{8}$ c. blueberries

Directions

1. Blend together cream cheese and honey with a hand mixer.
2. Scoop cream cheese mixture into a piping bag or a re-sealable plastic bag. If you're using a plastic bag, cut off a small tip of the bag.
3. Pipe cream cheese mixture into mini pie crusts.
4. Arrange fruit on top.

Chef's Note

Using a re-sealable plastic bag is an alternative way to pipe if you don't own a piping bag. This is a great dessert that is small but has just enough sweetness to satisfy a sweet tooth.

Fruit Salsa with Cinnamon Chips
Serves 4

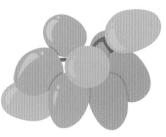

Ingredients

For the Fruit Salsa:
 1 c. diced strawberries
½ c. halved green grapes
½ c. diced pear
⅛ c. mint, cut into a chiffonade
½ c. sugar-free strawberry fruit
    preserves

For the Cinnamon Chips:
 4 small whole wheat tortillas
    Non-stick cooking spray
½ c. brown sugar
 1 tsp. cinnamon

Directions

For the Fruit Salsa:
1. Combine all of the ingredients in a large bowl and mix well.
2. Serve with Cinnamon Chips.

For the Cinnamon Chips:
1. Preheat oven to 350 degrees.
2. Spray tortillas on both sides with non-stick cooking spray.
3. In a small bowl, combine brown sugar and cinnamon. Sprinkle evenly over tortillas.
4. Cut tortillas into quarters.
5. Place on a baking sheet. Bake for 10 minutes or until golden brown.

56

Chef's Note

The ingredients in this sweet salsa have the colors of regular salsa. You can make it the night before and store it in an airtight container in the refrigerator. This is a perfect after-school snack!

Fruit Salsa with Cinnamon Chips

Inside-Out Peach Crumble

Inside-Out Peach Crumble
Serves 8

Ingredients

½ c. pecans
⅓ c. wheat flour
⅓ c. light brown sugar
1½ tbsp. canola oil
4 ripe peaches, halved and pitted

Directions

1. Preheat oven to 350 degrees.
2. Blend the pecans, flour, brown sugar, and canola oil in a food processor until it forms a coarse crumble.
3. Place the peach halves in muffin tins.
4. Add pecan mixture in the cavity of the peach halves.
5. Bake in the oven for 20 minutes or until fruit is tender and topping is golden.

Chef's Note

You can also use this technique with any large fruit that bakes well and can be scooped out, such as apples, nectarines, or pears.

Watermelon and Pineapple Pops

Serves 8-10

Ingredients

4 c. seedless watermelon, chopped
2 c. pineapple, chopped
1 tbsp. lemon juice
4 tbsp. honey

Directions

1. Using a food processor, blend all ingredients
   together so that they are combined but still slightly chunky.
2. Pour into popsicle molds.
3. Freeze until solid.

Chef's Note

Lemon and honey complement each other, and they also go well with fruit. These pops are sweet and healthy. They are also cool on a hot day!

Watermelon and Pineapple Pops

Glossary of Cooking Terms

Blanche—To briefly immerse in boiling water to soften an ingredient.

Blend—To thoroughly combine ingredients with a spoon or machine.

Butterfly—To cut ingredients open and spread flat.

Chiffonade—To slice herbs or leafy greens into thin, uniform strips, usually by rolling them up before cutting.

Chop—To cut food into uniform pieces.

Coat—To cover the surface of an ingredient with a fine substance such as flour.

Combine—To mix ingredients together.

Crumble—To break food into smaller pieces using your hands.

Dice—To cut food into small, uniform squares.

Drizzle—To pour a liquid in thin streams.

Fillet—To remove bones from the flesh of a meat.

Garnish—To add an edible item to a plate to make it more appealing.

Grate—To rub ingredients against a grater to create shreds.

Julienne—To cut food into thin, long strips about the size of a matchstick.

Marinate—To soak meat, fish, or other ingredients in a sauce.

Massage—To knead or rub meat to make it tender.

Mince—To chop ingredients into tiny pieces.

Peel—To remove the skin of a fruit or vegetable.

Pipe—To squeeze a mixture onto a surface using a pastry bag.

Pulse—To repeatedly turn a food processor on and off, resulting in a coarse mixture.

Quarter—To cut food into fourths.

Reduce—To boil down to a smaller volume.

Sauté—To cook food in a small amount of hot fat.

Shock—To place in ice water after ingredients have been blanched in order to stop cooking and preserve color.

Shred—To tear or cut into long, thin pieces.

Slice—To cut ingredients into even thicknesses.

Soften—To warm ingredients to room temperature and make malleable.

Sprinkle—To scatter dry ingredients or drops of liquid.

Stir—To mix ingredients in a circular motion.

Whisk—To beat rapidly with an instrument that allows air into the mixture, making it light and frothy. Also the name of a cooking tool used for this purpose.

Acknowledgments

Love to my family and mentors: Chef José Andrés, Chef John Besh, Chef Scott Boswell, Nina Camacho, Dr. Laney Chouest, Holly Clegg, Chef Gale Gand, Chef Eden Grinshpan, Mike Halsey, Jimmy Hornbeak, Chef Lala, Fe Reyes, Chef Aarón Sanchez, SoFab Institute, Tanya Steel, Chef Vaughn Trannon, VoiceAmerica Kids, and Andrew Zimmern. You add zest to my life!

The word "Pelican" and the depiction of a pelican are trademarks of Pelican Publishing Company, Inc., and are registered in the U.S. Patent and Trademark Office.

Library of Congress Cataloging-in-Publication Data

Kid Chef Eliana, 2000-
    Cool kids cook. Fresh and fit / by Kid Chef Eliana with Dianne de Las Casas ; illustrated by Soleil Lisette.
        pages cm.
    Age 8 to 12.
    ISBN 978-1-4556-1892-7 (hardcover : alkaline paper) — ISBN 978-1-4556-1893-4 (e-book) 1. International cooking—Juvenile literature. 2. Low-fat diet—Recipes—Juvenile literature. 3. Children—Nutrition—Juvenile literature. I. De Las Casas, Dianne. II. Lisette, Soleil, illustrator. III. Title. IV. Title: Fresh and fit.
    TX725.A1K48 2014
    641.5'622—dc23

                                                2013029809

Photography, prop, and food styling by Dianne de Las Casas and Kid Chef Eliana

Printed in Malaysia
Published by Pelican Publishing Company, Inc.
1000 Burmaster Street, Gretna, Louisiana 70053

You'll Need:

saucepan

casserole dish

cast iron skillet

 wok

 immersion blender

liquid measuring cup